Science of Cooking in the Kitchen

Children's Science & Nature

BABY PROFESSOR

EDUCATION KIDS

Speedy Publishing LLC
40 E. Main St. #1156
Newark, DE 19711
www.speedypublishing.com

The kitchen is a great place to explore science. Something simple like melting chocolate demonstrates how heat can change a substance from a solid to a liquid. You can create some science magic, bake, cook, set up a sensory activity, set up lava lamps and volcanoes or even play with ice. There are endless opportunities to learn in the kitchen.

Here are some things to do in the kitchen that can help you explore science:

Wet and Dry Things

This is to investigate the difference between wet and dry things.

Things you need:

Water
Various materials
like dried fruit, rice,
sponges, wash
cloths, pasta, cereal,
stone
Non-transparent
waterproof bag
Some small pots

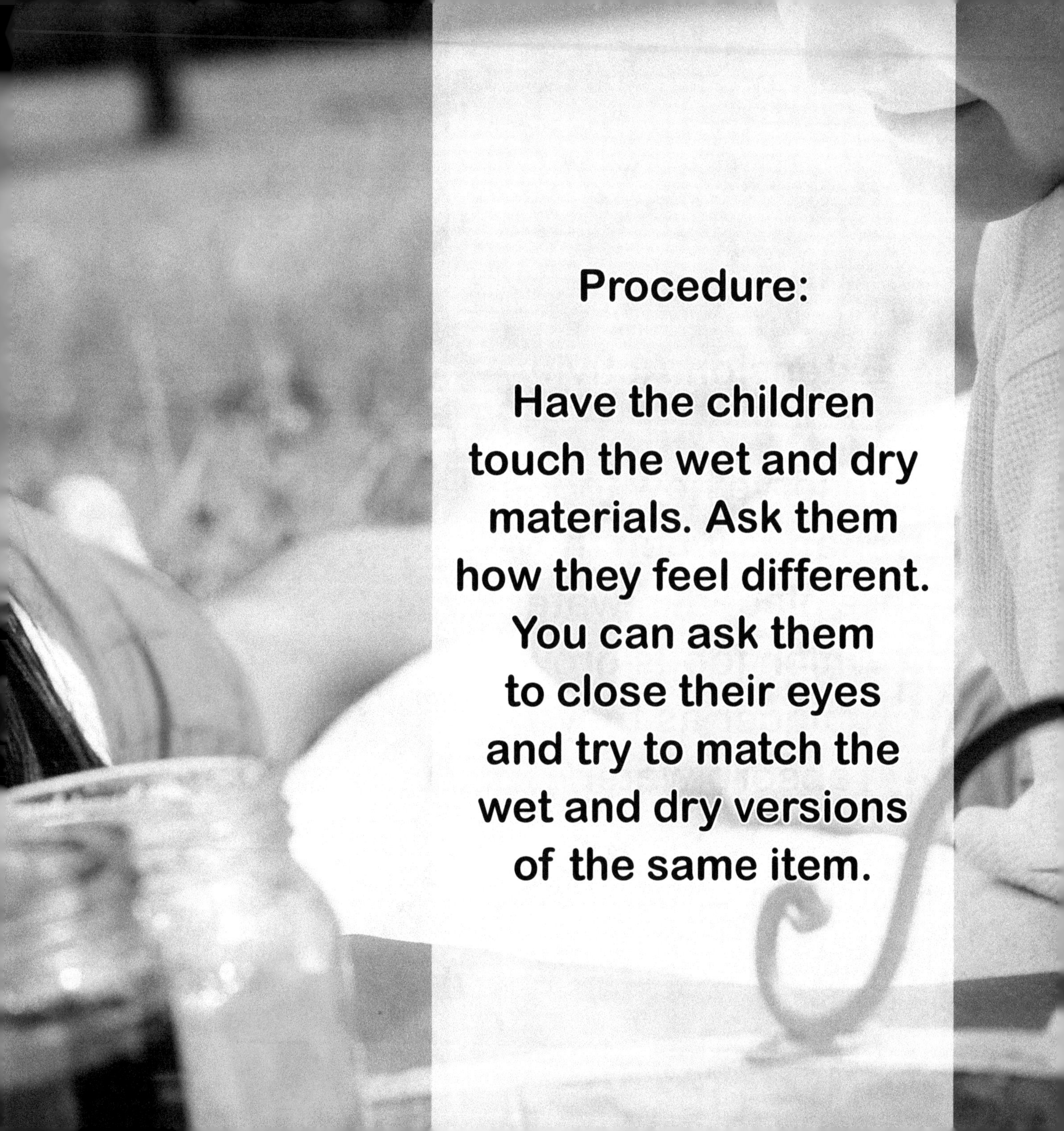

Procedure:

Have the children touch the wet and dry materials. Ask them how they feel different. You can ask them to close their eyes and try to match the wet and dry versions of the same item.

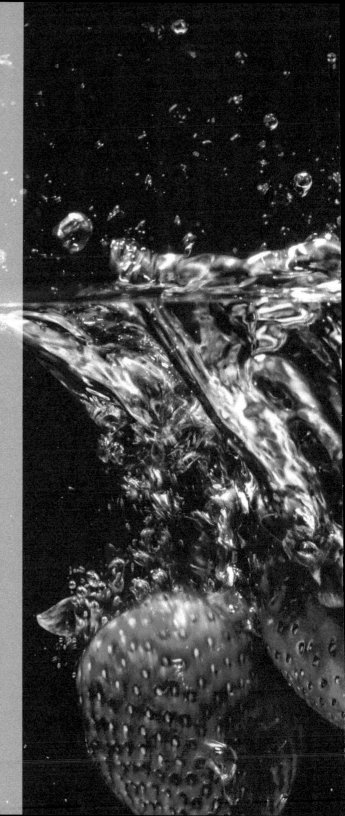

Extension Activity

Observe how foods change when they are placed in water. Which foods grow bigger as they absorb water?

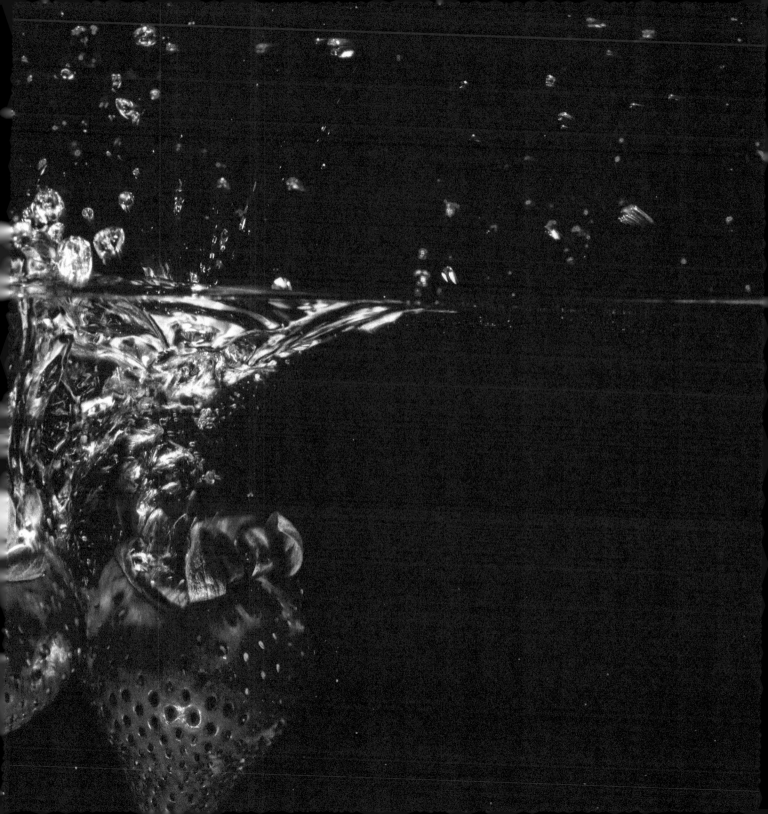

Density Experiment

Things you need:

Water
Molasses
Vegetable Oil
Corn Syrup
Food coloring
Small items to test
for floating
Large glass
A small glass

Procedure:

Put some water in the small glass, and add a few drops of food coloring.
Add liquids to the big glass in the following order. Start slowly with the molasses, then add the corn syrup, then the water and food coloring from the small glass. Finally, add the vegetable oil.
Drop a few small items in. Observe at which layer they float.

For example: a plastic bug will float on the top, a LEGO brick will float on the water and a paper clip will float on the molasses. Why is this so? Because of the differences in the weight of the items and the differences in the density of the liquids.

From Egg White to Meringue

In this experiment, we look at how the albumen or egg white transforms as you whisk it. Two thirds of the weight of an egg is the egg white. The egg white is mostly water, with 10% protein.

Things you need:

44 teaspoons white sugar
4 egg whites
Baking sheet
Parchment paper
2 baking sheets
A whisk
2 bowls
Tablespoon

A smaller number of
eggs can be used as long
as, for each egg white,
you use 55g of sugar.

Procedure:

Pre-heat the oven to 140 degrees.

Put parchment paper on the baking sheets.

Carefully separate the eggs, putting the egg whites in one bowl and the yolks in another bowl. Put the yolks away to use in a meal later. Whisk the eggs whites, slowly at first then faster as they expand. The egg whites are ready once you get stiff peaks.

Slowly add sugar, a few tablespoons each time. Make sure that after each addition of sugar, whisk the mixture again.

Use the tablespoon to put the mixture onto the baking sheets, leaving spaces between the spoonfuls.

Place the baking sheets on the lower shelf in the oven. Bake for about 45 minutes. Turn off the oven, but leave the meringue inside for another 15 minutes.

You may serve this with whipped cream and fruit.

What we Learned

Two things happen when we whisk egg whites:

The act of whisking creates a force that unfolds the protein molecules in the egg white.

Foam is made as the air bubbles get into the unfolded proteins during the whisking.

As the mixture bakes, the foam hardens into meringue.

From the experiments above, you can have fun learning about science. There are many more simple experiments that can be done in the kitchen.

Printed in the USA
CPSIA information can be obtained
at www.ICGtesting.com
LVHW080508151023
761011LV00014B/137